# WELCOME TO JEDBURGH ABBEY

T he abbey of St Mary stands on an elevated position overlooking the Jed Water in Jedburgh. It probably occupies the site of an earlier religious community; indeed this spot may have been the focus of Christian worship in Jedburgh for more than 1,000 years.

Founded around 1138 by King David I and Bishop John of Glasgow, this major Augustinian abbey is one of the most complete in Scotland. The scale and quality of its buildings, and their location close to the border with England, were clear statements of David's ambitions for the Scottish church, and even today the abbey presents an awesome visual delight to visitors approaching from the south. It was a spiritual place, where the canons offered prayers perpetually in the hope of eternal salvation. The abbey's location close to the border, however, led to a turbulent history.

**Right:** A view of the nave through the east processional doorway.

**Opposite:** Inside the south choir chapel.

## CONTENTS

**Picture:** A painting of the abbey by J.M.W. Turner, dated 1832.

## GRAND DESIGNS

### 11 THE EAST END
Originally built with two tiers of sturdy Romanesque piers, but later rebuilt and extended in Gothic style, with a third tier, or clearstory, above.

### 14 THE NAVE
The three-tiered western limb of the abbey church is a wonderfully light and ornate arrangement of Gothic arches.

### 15 THE WEST FAÇADE
A magnificent decorative front with the processional entrance and the later rose window as its most prominent features.

## FINER DETAILS

### 12 BISHOPS' SIGNATURES
Rebuilding work in the 1400s was commissioned by successive bishops, who had their heraldic devices or initials carved into the masonry.

### 15 THE ROSE WINDOW
Inserted in the 1400s when the gable was redesigned, the rose window has retained its elegance.

### 16 CARVED DOORWAYS
Aside from the west façade, the nave has two ornately carved doorways leading out to the cloister. One is original, the other a Victorian reconstruction.

# JEDBURGH ABBEY AT A GLANCE

Home to a community of Augustinian canons for over 400 years, Jedburgh Abbey contains some of the finest Romanesque and Gothic architecture anywhere in Scotland.

**Below:** The soaring west façade of the abbey church.

The abbey church is among the most complete in the country, and it stands alongside the more ruinous canons' domestic buildings, arranged around a cloister in a plan customary for a religious establishment. The domestic ranges were the focus of a major archaeological investigation in 1984, which revealed much new information about the form of these buildings and shed light on the everyday lives of the canons who inhabited them.

By founding the abbey here, David I was demonstrating that his control extended up to the border with England and that the Scots were able to build on the grand scale. Although founded in peaceful times, the abbey's location eventually exposed it to conflict, but even after the Protestant Reformation of 1560, it continued to be an important religious focus for the local community.

## PLEASANT SURROUNDINGS

### 7 THE JED WATER
The river not only supplied water for the canons' needs, but was channelled into a lade to power a grain mill and later mills for wool and snuff.

### 16 THE CLOISTER GARDEN
Replanted in 1986, the garden grows herbs and other plants that would have been used by the canons for both culinary and medicinal purposes.

### 18 THE ORCHARD
An orchard has also been planted, beyond the mill lade. 'Jethart' pears grown here were once sold as far afield as London.

## PRECIOUS ARTEFACTS

### 22 THE COMB
Perhaps the most enigmatic object found during the 1984 excavations, the 'Jedburgh comb' dates from around 1100.

### 22 THE SHRINE
An elaborately carved shrine, dated to the early 700s but very well preserved, can be seen in the visitor centre.

### 23 THE ROMAN ALTARS
Two inscribed Roman altar panels were found at the abbey – one within the fabric of the nave. Both are thought to have come from the fort at nearby Cappuck.

# A SHORT TOUR OF JEDBURGH ABBEY

This short tour guides you around the abbey, highlighting the architectural and archaeological features of interest. It follows the same route as the on-site audio tour.

An exhibition in the visitor centre introduces the abbey and displays some of the most remarkable artefacts discovered here. A model of the abbey as it might have appeared at the beginning of the 1500s offers a further insight into the scale and grandeur of the abbey's buildings when complete.

From the visitor centre, one can contemplate the form and scale of the abbey. The complex of buildings is set on a slope, with the abbey church at the highest part, at the north of the site so that it did not block the light from the domestic ranges in front. Before building work could commence, the sloping ground above the Jed Water had to be levelled in order to create platforms for the buildings arranged around the cloister. Stone had to be quarried, probably from Ulston Moor, over a mile away, and carried to the site. It is not surprising then that the original abbey took over 100 years to complete.

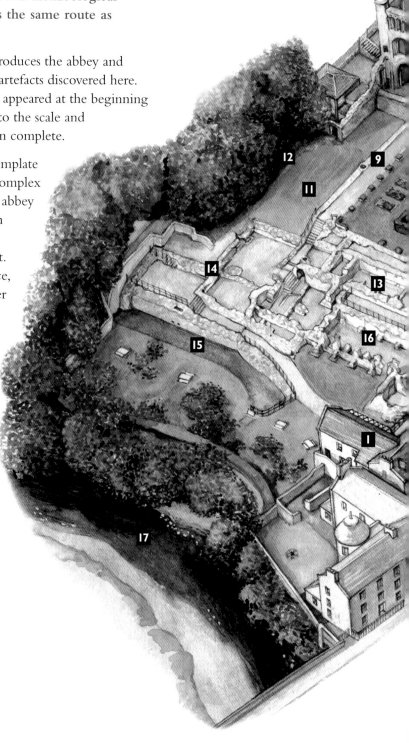

**Key**

| | | | |
|---|---|---|---|
| 1 | Visitor centre | 10 | Cloister garden |
| 2 | East range cellars | 11 | Site of west range |
| 3 | Chapter house | 12 | Site of manse |
| 4 | South transept | 13 | Site of refectory |
| 5 | East end | 14 | Site of kitchens |
| 6 | Tower | 15 | Great drain (later lade) |
| 7 | North transept | 16 | Site of abbot's lodging |
| 8 | Nave | 17 | Jed Water |
| 9 | Cloister | | |

**Below:** Medieval masons at work.

**Bottom:** An artist's impression of the abbey complex as it may have looked in the late 1300s.

Temporary wooden structures, providing accommodation for both canons and builders, were built first, but thereafter the church was the focus of early building work. Construction of the east and south cloister ranges followed, and finally the west range was built to complete the cloister. Due to the sloping ground, the south range had to be raised on a massively constructed undercroft, or cellars, to bring it level with the cloister.

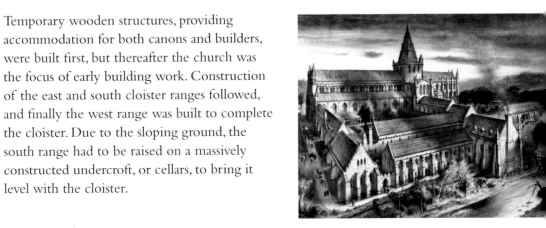

5

**Left:** The abbey church around 1880. At this time, much of the abbey complex was built over.

**Below:** The excavations of 1984, which revealed much of the complex as we see it today. The east range cellars are in the centre foreground.

# CELLARS OF THE EAST RANGE

The vaulted undercroft or cellars of the east range were built in the early 1200s, and the ashlar-lined walls still retain remnants of finely-carved blind arcading. The dark, cool conditions made the cellars ideal for storage.

A large storage space would have been important, particularly for storing sufficient food to provide for the abbey's community over the winter months. Two floors above the cellars was the canons' dormitory, which had a night-stair at its northern end, leading into the south transept, making access to early-morning services easier. At its southern end was the toilet block, or reredorter. The reredorter emptied into a drain flushed by water channelled from the nearby Jed Water.

The storeys above the undercroft appear to have suffered a catastrophic failure, possibly due to war damage, and archaeological evidence reveals that the undercroft was abandoned little more than a century after it was built. A crude wall was built across part of it, and its southern half became a free-standing building. This area was eventually occupied by a grain mill, its wheel driven by the water that had previously flushed the drains. The mill lade, diverted from the Jed Water and running from west to east, can be seen passing beneath the visitor centre. The lower part of its northern wall is of medieval date and contains the outlet of the abbey's west drain.

After the Reformation of 1560, much of the east range was demolished, and three houses were built on top of the remains. One of these was later converted for use as a smithy. The southern part of the east range continued in light industrial use, mostly milling, long after the last canon died. The mill lade continued to provide power for new woollen mills on the site of the old corn mill, and to a snuff mill to the east of the abbey. The last of these mills closed down in the 1960s.

## DID YOU KNOW . . .

One of the most remarkable finds excavated in this area is a merelles board, carved in stone. Also known as nine men's morris, merelles is a game for two players in which each attempts to place three counters in a line, thus gaining one of the opponent's counters. At some point, the board was used as building material and incorporated into the fabric of the south range.

# THE CHAPTER HOUSE

Aside from the church, the chapter house was the most important building in the abbey. It served as the canons' principal meeting place. They gathered here each day to hear a reading from the rule of St Augustine (see page 27), to be given news and instructions and to confess their sins.

**Above:** The wall footings of the east range.

Excavations in 1984 identified three distinct phases in the development of this building. The original structure had projected a short distance to the east of the other east range buildings, suggesting that it may have been built first. The first chapter house was not provided with stone seats, at least on its north side, since burials were found right up to that wall. Later, the chapter house was extended eastwards, presumably reflecting an increase in the size of the community. This larger chapter house is marked out by edge stones. In the late 1400s, by which time the community had decreased in size, the chapter house was reduced to the present square chamber, a development paralleled elsewhere in Scotland at Glenluce Abbey in Galloway and Crossraguel Abbey in Ayrshire. The base of a pillar, which once supported a cross-ribbed vault, is prominent at the centre of the building.

The chapter house was a favoured place of burial for senior officials of the abbey and for important benefactors. The 1984 excavations provided insights into life and death in the abbey. Examination of the bones revealed cases of degenerative diseases such as osteoarthritis and periostitis, and one individual may have suffered from gout. There was at least one example of a dental abscess so severe it caused the deterioration of the bone around it. Following careful examination, the human remains were re-interred in the chapter house, during an ecumenical service involving all the congregations in Jedburgh.

## THE PARLOUR

The small, vaulted passage, or slype, to the north of the chapter house led to the canons' burial ground to the east. This structure may have served as the parlour, where limited conversation was permitted between the brethren, who were otherwise vowed to silence.

## THE WARMING HOUSE

The room immediately to the south of the chapter house may have served as the warming house, or calefactory, where the canons were permitted to gather around the hearth on cold winter days, but only for short periods. On the floor above the chapter house, parlour and warming house was the canons' dormitory.

**Above right:** The chapter house at Glenluce Abbey, built in a similar style to the one at Jedburgh.

**Right:** Skeletons discovered below the chapter house provide evidence of its use for important burials.

# THE ABBEY CHURCH

The church was the focus of life in the abbey. The prime purpose of the canons' lives was to dedicate themselves to God and to the teaching of his word.

Like most major churches of the medieval period, Jedburgh abbey church was laid out in a cruciform or cross-shaped plan, with its head towards the east.

At the east end lay the presbytery, containing the high altar. In front of this was the canons' choir, stretching below the tower and into the east end of the nave. The arms of the cross were formed by the transepts, projecting on either side of the choir. The shaft of the cross formed the nave, where the lay people worshipped. The eastern end of the church provides an excellent comparison between the monumental strength of the Romanesque work of 1138 and the delicate Gothic of 40 years later. The quality of the church architecture reveals the innovation and ingenuity of the builders.

**Below:** The abbey church viewed from the NW.

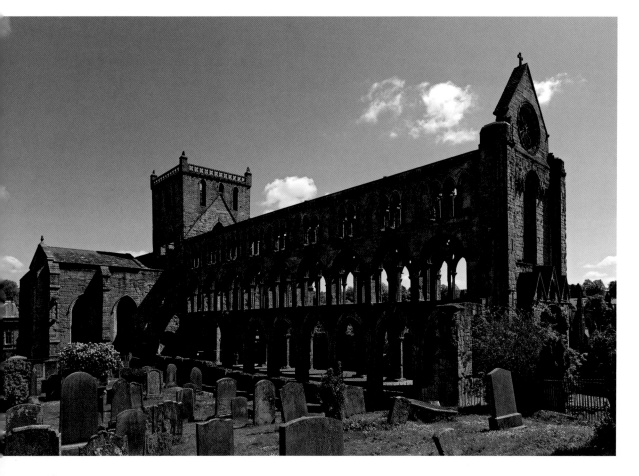

# THE EAST END

As the spiritual heart of the abbey, the east end of the church, housing the high altar, was the first part to be built. It was important that its design should reflect its status as well as meeting its functional needs.

Several services were held before the high altar each day. The canons also found time for prayer and private dedication at additional altars. The high altar was centrally placed at the east end of the church in the presbytery. Extra altars were provided within the transepts, in the choir-aisle chapels and in the nave. The original transepts had apsidal east ends and extended a single bay in width.

There is evidence of at least three phases of development within the present east end. The 1138 church was built in the Romanesque style and can be best seen in the choir elevations. They have an unusual arrangement of giant, column-like piers with scalloped caps, which rise through both the arcade and the gallery. This work was clearly carried out by an experienced master mason, who may have been brought to Jedburgh from either Tewkesbury in Gloucestershire or Reading in Berkshire.

The design of the choir at Jedburgh may have been inspired by that of a group of churches in southern and western England. Romsey Abbey in Hampshire, built in the early 1100s, is the best surviving example. King David would have been familiar with Romsey, as his aunt, Christina, was a nun there, and he visited his sister, Matilda, in the abbey when she was staying there before her marriage to Henry I.

The original presbytery was shorter than the present layout. It probably had a lower storey consisting of an arcade of engaged arches, perhaps akin to those in the abbey church at Kelso. Above were round-topped windows. It was roofed over with a timber ceiling, probably a wagon vault.

**Left:** An artist's impression of the east end as it may have looked on completion of the first phase.

# DEVELOPING THE EAST END

The second phase began around 1180. The presbytery was rebuilt and extended, but there was no attempt to match the new architecture with the existing work.

To light it, new slender windows were set into an elegant arcade of alternate high and low pointed arches. Below it was an arcade of engaged, decorated, pointed arches.

The final phase of work was the building of a clearstory. A low clearstory was added to the east end of the church first. This was replaced with a taller clearstory over the presbytery and choir (leaving the low clearstory in the transepts). This was not completed until some time in the 1200s.

When finished, the choir and presbytery were used by the canons without disruption until the early 1400s. Rebuilding was perhaps prompted by war damage, or there may have been a need to increase the number of altars. The first major works involved the reconstruction of the north transept to a larger rectangular plan. Its eastern wall was left blank to house elaborate altar-pieces, and the space was lit by large traceried windows in the north and west walls. It was probably built at the request of Bishop Turnbull of Glasgow, who was also responsible for some alterations to the chapel on the south side of the choir; his coat of arms appears on one of the buttresses here. The English attack of 1464 necessitated a major reconstruction of the crossing area, when the southern piers beneath the tower were rebuilt and strengthened.

**Above:** The presbytery as it looks today.

## THE LOTHIAN AISLE

The north transept was adopted as a burial place by the Ker family, ancestors of the present owners, the marquises of Lothian. It contains tombs and memorials ranging in date from 1524, when Sir Andrew Ker of Fernieherst, Lord Warden of the Marches, was buried there, to the present day.

**Below:** The initials of Abbot Thomas Cranston, who commissioned the reconstruction of the tower in the 1480s.

Following this, the tower was reconstructed and a barrel vault added to the south transept. The heraldic devices of those who commissioned the work, Abbots John Hall (1478–84) and Thomas Cranston (1484–8), and Archbishop Robert Blacader of Glasgow, were incorporated into the stonework. The last of the medieval works visible at the east end demonstrate damage limitation on a tragic scale when the community was spiritually and financially exhausted. The crudely-built walls and lowered roofs represent a desperate attempt to maintain a church in the crossing area. It is even possible that the community abandoned their dormitory, and used the upper areas of the tower and transepts as safe accommodation after the attack of 1523.

Repairs to the church were only just complete when the attacks of 1544 and 1545 dealt the final blow. After that, the community seems only to have managed to block off and abandon the south transept in the hope that, in the future, they might be able to repair it. However, the Reformation intervened and the truncated church in the crossing became the parish church of Jedburgh.

**Left:** An artist's impression of the east end as it may have looked on completion of the clearstory in the 1200s.

# THE NAVE

T he nave was the only part of the abbey open to lay people. It is remarkable for its structural completeness, giving us an unparalleled impression of a medieval abbey church.

The nave was begun in the 1180s, but not completed until early in the following century. It was planned on a grand scale: divided into nine bays flanked by an aisle on each side and three storeys in height. The nave arcade has richly-moulded arches carried on eight-lobed piers topped with elegant capitals. Above these, the galleries have round-arched openings subdivided with two pointed arches in each bay, and above them the clearstory provided light for the nave with two windows in a continuous arcade of four arches to each bay.

The appearance of the whole is light and airy, with the mass of stone effortlessly supported – the very opposite of the strength and solidity found in the Romanesque elevations in the choir. Subtle differences exist in the carving of the capitals and the forming of the vaults over the aisles, which suggest the nave was built from west to east. Stairs built into the west wall permit a fine view along the nave. The west wall also features a magnificent processional doorway.

**Top left:** The nave viewed from the tower.

**Top centre:** The view along the nave from the gallery in the west wall.

**Top right:** The three tiers of the nave seen from the south nave aisle.

## THE 17TH-CENTURY PARISH CHURCH

When the parish church within the crossing was declared dangerous in the late 1600s, a new church was constructed in the five western bays of the nave (at the right of the picture). A gallery was inserted at the west end, accessed via the enlarged window in the south side of the west wall. The roof sprang from the top of the gallery and was entirely within the height of the earlier nave. The entrance to the church was through the west door and a door in the north wall which was provided with an external porch.

The west front's elevation is so similar to that at Kelso Abbey that it is tempting to suppose it is the work of the same masons. The richly carved doorway is surmounted by three gablet niches which once held statues. The single tall window above was flanked by an elegant arcade and above is the gable, rebuilt in the 1400s, when the handsome rose window was inserted. At the east and west ends of the nave's south wall are arched doorways leading out to the cloister.

**Far left:** An engraving of the west front dated 10 July 1790.

**Left:** A similar view by W.H. Lizars, dated 1832.

**Bottom left:** Another view of the west front by R.W. Billings, around 1850.

# THE CLOISTER

At the centre of the abbey, the cloister was a rectangular open area, defined on all sides by imposing buildings. It had a covered walkway around its perimeter.

The cloister walkway served as far more than a protected corridor connecting the various parts of the abbey. The canons used it as a processional route during important services, and on an everyday basis as a space for reading, writing and contemplation.

The doorways at the east and west ends of the nave's south wall connected with the cloister and acted as processional doorways into the church. The east doorway is a fine example of the mason's craft of the 1180s; the western doorway is a reconstruction dating from 1876. In the mid-1300s, the original cloister was extended to the south and west.

**Above:** The cloister garden. The juniper tree at the centre was due to be replaced when this photograph was taken.

## THE GARDEN

The central part of the cloister may have served as a garden, tended by the canons. It has been laid out once again as a late-medieval garden. Flowers, shrubs and herbs of the period grow here. These include plants cultivated for their medicinal or culinary properties. During the medieval period, monastic establishments played a leading role in developing gardening skills and advancing medical science through the application of herbal remedies. The Augustinians were at the forefront of medical research.

The canons were self-sufficient in many ways, growing vegetables, fruit and pot herbs for the refectory table, medicinal herbs for the infirmary and flowers for the church altars.

The square, gravelled court defined by yew hedging indicates the extent of the first cloister, laid out in the early 1100s. At the centre of the garden is a juniper, which represented the Tree of Life. In the five radiating flower beds are flowers and plants that would have been well-known to the early canons, including damask rose, hyssop, alkanet and cotton lavender. No doubt the cloister garden was also valued as a refuge from the hustle and bustle of the abbey, and was used for quiet contemplation.

### DID YOU KNOW ...

The yew tree, which could bear heavy weights of snow, was used as a protective cover and came to symbolise immortality.

**Top left:** Bluebells in the cloister garden.

**Left:** The restored cloister at Iona Abbey. Jedburgh's cloister may have had a similar arrangement of roofing and pillars.

# THE WEST AND SOUTH RANGES

The west range of the complex consisted of those buildings which required contact with the outside world. Although this part of the site is now in ruins, enough has survived to give an impression of the abbey's scale. The main building in the south range was the refectory.

Rooms in the west range would have included an outer parlour, where the canons could occasionally meet their families. There would also have been rooms for the cellarer, responsible for provisions, the almoner, who looked after the poor at the gate, and the guest master, who provided hospitality for travellers.

After the Reformation, probably in the 1600s, the west range was rebuilt to form a manse for the minister of the post-Reformation church. This survived on the site until 1876, when both church and manse were relocated to a new site across the Jed Water. The original manse's well still survives.

On the south side of the cloister was the canons' dining hall or refectory. At some stage, perhaps after the English raids of the early 1300s, the canons extended the cloister to the west and south. This involved constructing a new west range and re-routing the south cloister walk through the range itself, while the refectory was relocated above the walkway and a narrow undercroft. Nothing now remains of the refectory, but a drain which served the canons' washing place, or lavatory, survives. At the west end of the refectory are the remains of the kitchens.

To the south of the south range, between the refectory and the river, is an undercroft of 13th-century date. The high quality of its architecture suggests that it may have formed part of the abbot's lodging. In this location the abbot could be seen to be living communally with the canons, but with the independence his status expected of him.

## THE ORCHARD
To the south of the mill lade, a small orchard has been planted. The fruit trees here provide a further flavour of the richness of garden produce available to the brethren. Jedburgh was for a long time famous for the quality of its pears, apples and plums; indeed the 'Jethart' pears were a favourite fruit on the streets of London and Newcastle in recent centuries and a source of considerable income for their growers. It is likely that fruits such as these were among the food stored by the medieval canons in the dark, cool cellars of the east range.

**Above:** The south range, with the abbey church in the background.

**Far left:** The probable site of the abbot's lodging. Part of the undercroft is all that remains.

**Left:** A view towards the orchard.

# THE STORY OF
# JEDBURGH
# ABBEY

Jedburgh Abbey was founded jointly by King David I and Bishop John of Glasgow, his former tutor, no later than 1138. They chose what had almost certainly been the site of a Christian establishment since the 9th century.

The site's past as a religious centre was clearly significant. But perhaps more importantly, the king wanted to demonstrate to Scots and English alike that he was able to build on a magnificent scale at the very fringe of the kingdom.

Although initially founded as a priory, the Augustinian house had been elevated to the status of an abbey by 1154, and grew to become one of the most significant religious houses in Scotland.

The abbey's location near the Border made it particularly susceptible to attack, and on numerous occasions it suffered damage from military action and was repaired. In the 1540s, however, the level of devastation proved decisive and the abbey never recovered. The Reformation in 1560 witnessed the final decline. However, the parishioners continued to use the abbey church until the late 1800s, enabling it to survive roofless but otherwise almost complete.

**Opposite:** An engraving by R.W. Billings, around 1850, shows the arcades forming the nave.

**Right:** A crudely carved Christian stone found at the site. It has been dated to the 9th or 10th century.

TIMELINE

| 830 | 1059 |

BISHOP ECRED OF LINDISFARNE
establishes a church at Gedwearde (Jedburgh), which may already have been a sacred site.

THE AUGUSTINIANS
are recognised as an order following St Augustine of Hippo (345–430).

# THE EARLY CHURCH

J edburgh has had a long association with Christianity. When Bishop Ecgred of Lindisfarne built a church at Gedwearde (Jedworth) in 830, the site may already have been known for its Christian associations.

One of the finest shrine fragments in Scotland comes from in or near Jedburgh and is dated to the early 8th century. A shrine of such quality could only have been created for someone of great wealth or sanctity and must surely have been housed within a church. Several other fragments of early Christian stones, along with Anglo-Saxon coins, have also been found in the vicinity of the abbey.

The precise site of the early church established by Ecgred is not known, although we know that he founded two settlements within a few miles of each other, both called Jedworth. Indeed, little is known about the religious community here until around 1080, when Eadulph Rus, implicated in the murder of Bishop Walcher of Durham, was buried in the church. His remains were later unceremoniously dug up and disposed of.

Objects discovered by archaeologists provide tantalising glimpses of the site's early history. Many of these support the idea of Jedburgh as a Christian establishment, though there are also secular objects.

The 'Jedburgh comb' was discovered during major excavations of the site in 1984. Carved from a single piece of walrus ivory and measuring only 50mm in length, it was found in a ditch to the east of the chapter house.

**Right:** Part of a beautifully carved and extraordinarily well preserved shrine found at Jedburgh, dated to the 8th century.

Just inside the entrance to the stairway in the NW corner of the nave, a Roman altar has been re-used as a lintel. Its Latin inscription translates as, 'To Jupiter, best and greatest, the detachment of Raetian spearmen, under the acting command of Julius Severinus, their tribune [set this up]'. Part of the inscribed face of another Roman altar (right), was re-used as a paving stone in the abbey. It can be seen in the visitor centre. Both stones may have come from the Roman fort at Cappuck, 4 miles east of Jedburgh.

**Above:** A drawing of the inscribed face of a Roman altar panel, later used as a paving stone.
**Below:** The Jedburgh comb, dating from around 1100.

The comb displays a superb level of craftsmanship, and its panels are decorated with scenes depicting a knight fighting with a dragon on one side, and a griffin attacking an animal on the other. A late-11th or early-12th-century date is thought likely for this object, which was probably used to comb the beard or moustache of an aristocratic owner.

The comb was found in close association with other artefacts; a ceramic lamp, a cooking pot, a seal pendant (also of walrus ivory), a buckle, probably of horn, and a whetstone. These were all found beside the articulated upper torso of a man, probably a murder victim. While it is tempting to link this discovery to the story of Eadulph Rus, the circumstances and dating do not provide strong enough evidence of a connection.

## 1080

## AROUND 1100

**BISHOP WALCHER**
of Durham (left) is assassinated. The culprit, Eadwulf Rus, flees to Jedburgh, where he himself is murdered and buried.

**EADWULF RUS**
is exhumed from his grave at Jedburgh and his remains are thrown out of the church.

# THE AUGUSTINIAN FOUNDATION

Jedburgh Abbey was founded at a time of tremendous activity in the religious life of Scotland. Following a long period in which monastic life had almost disappeared, a succession of monarchs realised the advantages, both political and spiritual, of a vibrant national church.

David I and Bishop John were both genuinely pious, and under their influence the Scottish church embarked on a renewal. David had spent his youth at the court of his brother-in-law, Henry I of England. There, he had observed first-hand how the great religious houses had played their part alongside the royal castles in governing the population. Later, on his travels through Europe, he had become familiar with the blossoming new religious orders there and he was responsible for introducing several of these into Scotland.

The founding brethren were probably brought from St Quentin Abbey near Beauvais, northern France. David planned to reorganise the church in Scotland, and to loosen the grip of the Archbishop of York, who claimed authority over it. Endowing a religious community was very costly and David gave grants of royal property to an extent which was to dismay later kings.

**Above:** Illustration of an Augustinian canon from Sir William Dugdale's *Monasticon Anglicanum* (1655–73).

## DAVID I'S ABBEYS

At Jedburgh Abbey, King David showed that he was in a position to build on a grand scale, even on the edge of his kingdom.

David I was responsible for introducing several religious orders into Scotland and changing the political, social, economic and religious landscape of the country. He had a comprehensive knowledge of the emerging religious orders, and he was responsible for the very first reformed monastic house in Britain, when he founded a house for the Tironensian Order at Selkirk in 1113 (relocated to Kelso in the 1120s). He also established the greatest of the reformed orders, the Cistercians, at Melrose in 1136.

His other major monastic foundations include Cambuskenneth Abbey, Dunfermline Abbey (right), Holyrood Abbey (all now in Historic Scotland's care), Kinloss Abbey and Loch Leven Priory.

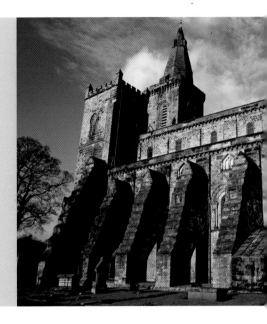

Other benefactors, both Scots and English, who wished to share the merits of supporting the canons' prayers, also made generous gifts. Some not only gave land but also donated parish churches, the income from which was appropriated by the canons. Before 1154, Jedburgh's status was raised to that of an abbey, and it increased in authority and wealth. Eventually, it came to have the priories at Blantyre in Lanarkshire, Canonbie in Dumfriesshire and Restenneth in Angus dependent upon it. By the Reformation, the abbey enjoyed a very considerable annual income.

**Below:** A medieval bone stylus found at Jedburgh. The sharp end was used by the canons to write, possibly in wax. The blunt end was used to erase errors.

**Opposite:** The abbey viewed from the NW.

### 1138

**DAVID I**
and his former tutor, Bishop John of Glasgow, found a new priory at Jedburgh. The founding brethren are Augustinians, probably from Beauvais, France.

### AROUND 1150

**JEDBURGH PRIORY**
is elevated in status to become an abbey.

# THE AUGUSTINIAN ORDER

The Augustinians took their name from St Augustine of Hippo. In the 11th century, groups of priests seeking a form of spiritual co-existence began looking to his teachings for guidance. When they were formally recognised as a distinct order in 1059 they adopted him as their figurehead.

The order encompassed a wide variety of spiritual ideals embracing almost every aspect of religious life. The 'black canons', as they were known from the colour of their habit, were not monks but priests, and were not as strictly organised as the orders of monks.

Although they lived a cloistered and contemplative life, they were not entirely cut off from the outside world, and they would often leave the abbey to preach in parishes. However, their lives were essentially monastic.

They were bound by the vows of poverty, chastity and obedience and their reason for retiring from the world was the same, to dedicate their lives to God.

Worship dominated their lives, and most of their days were spent in the cloister, attending the daily round of services of psalms, prayers and anthems, beginning in the early hours of the morning and ending in the early evening. There was also time for spiritual and intellectual activities, and manual work such as tending the gardens and preparing meals.

It is not clear why David selected the Augustinian order for Jedburgh. The Augustinian establishments were located close to the seats of government, like Holyrood, close to Edinburgh Castle and Cambuskenneth, near Stirling. This may reflect the importance of Augustinian abbots and priors to bureaucracy of government, in which they often served as clerks. The royal castle at Jedburgh was frequently visited by the royal court.

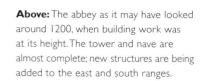

**Above:** The abbey as it may have looked around 1200, when building work was at its height. The tower and nave are almost complete; new structures are being added to the east and south ranges.

**Above:** The seal of Abbot Hugh, who ran the abbey around 1205–10.

## ST AUGUSTINE

St Augustine of Hippo (left) was born and raised in Roman north Africa. He is acknowledged as being an important influence on the development of western Christianity. A prolific writer, his surviving works include over 100 books and treatises, over 200 letters, and over 500 sermons. Perhaps his most famous work, *Confessions* is a long prayer of penitence and thanksgiving for the grace of God. Augustinian canons were pledged to observe St Augustine's rule. This was a set of instructions or precepts, based on the ideals of the earliest Christian communities. It drew on the concepts of humility, community, abstinence and prayer at set times throughout the day. St Augustine died in AD 430.

**Above:** A painting of St Augustine by El Greco.

## 1165

### MALCOLM IV
dies during a visit to Jedburgh Castle.

## 1170

### WILLIAM I
grants Jedburgh its first royal charter.

# THE ABBEY AND THE TOWN

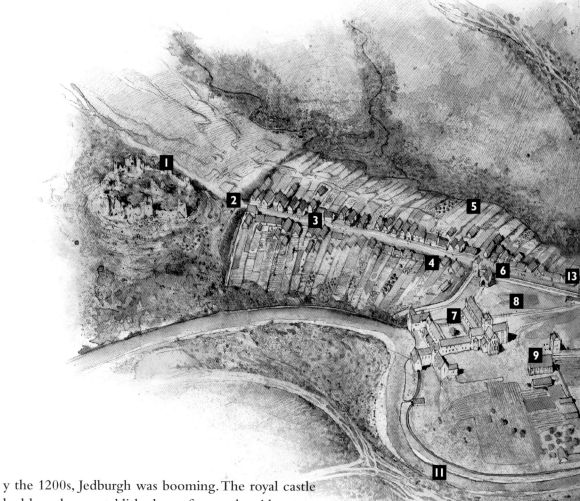

B y the 1200s, Jedburgh was booming. The royal castle had long been established as a favoured residence of the court, the abbey was wealthy and influential, and the royal burgh, first given a charter in 1170, was flourishing.

The burgh had developed in a cruciform plan with the main street running northward from the castle to a ford across the Jed Water leading to Bongate. The east–west road ran from another ford (close to the existing late-medieval Canongate Bridge), along Canongate and through the market place to a point on Burn Wynd where the road crossed the Skiprunning Burn. That burn and the Jed Water together formed the boundaries of the burgage plots and probably defined the town.

Each entrance point into the town was protected by a strong port, or gate, which served both to regulate trade and to defend the town. These were in addition to the gates protecting the abbey precinct itself, which previously occupied all of the land within the sweep of the Jed Water from Abbey Close to Canongate.

**Below:** A view of the abbey from south of the Jed Water.

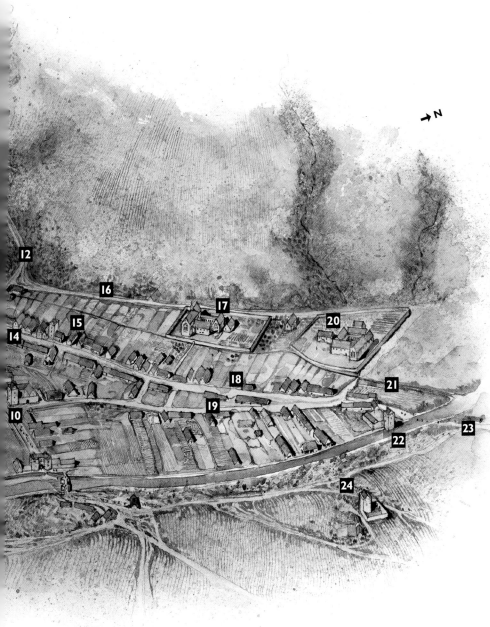

**Key**

| | |
|---|---|
| 1 | Castle (dismantled 1409) |
| 2 | Townhead Port |
| 3 | Townhead |
| 4 | Lawnmarket |
| 5 | Skiprunning Burn |
| 6 | Dabie's Tower |
| 7 | Abbey |
| 8 | Abbey precinct |
| 9 | St Ninian's Tower |
| 10 | Canongate |
| 11 | Jed Water |
| 12 | Burn Wynd |
| 13 | Market Place |
| 14 | Highgate |
| 15 | Moscrope's Tower |
| 16 | Back of Friars |
| 17 | Franciscan friary |
| 18 | Black Quarter |
| 19 | Backgate |
| 20 | Maison Dieu |
| 21 | Townfoot Port |
| 22 | Pyle's Walls |
| 23 | Bongate |
| 24 | Stone Hill |

**Left:** Jedburgh as it may have looked in the early 1500s.

## 1285

**ALEXANDER III** marries his second wife, Yolande de Dreux, at Jedburgh Abbey.

## 1296

**EDWARD I OF ENGLAND** launches his invasion of Scotland. At Jedburgh Abbey, he establishes a base and installs a pro-English abbot.

# THE ABBEY AT WAR

Jedburgh's location near the border with England made the abbey particularly susceptible to attack. It suffered damage from military action on numerous occasions. The level of devastation caused in the 1540s would prove decisive and the abbey never recovered.

In 1285, Alexander III married Yolande de Dreux in Jedburgh Abbey. Legend tells us that a ghostly figure appeared at the wedding, foretelling the king's death. He suffered a fatal accident the following year. This was followed in 1290 by the death of his heir, Margaret, the Maid of Norway, aged just seven. Then came the short reign of John Balliol (1292–6). All of this formed the prelude to the Wars of Independence with England.

Jedburgh became involved soon after the conflict began in 1296, when Edward I of England lodged in the abbey. During his stay he oversaw the election of a pro-English abbot, but this did not save the brethren from subsequent attacks, from both sides. In 1305 the lead was stripped from the roofs by English troops, possibly to make siege engines. Throughout the wars, the canons walked a political tightrope. Their leanings seem to have been towards the English and in 1307 Edward II wrote to Abbot William entreating him to remain loyal. By 1312, however, life had become intolerable for the community. The Scots had recaptured Roxburgh Castle and were threatening Jedburgh. Feeling vulnerable, the abbot and 11 canons fled across the Border to take refuge in Yorkshire. For the next decade at least, some of the community remained in exile.

**Right:** André de Montalembert, Comte d'Esse, who commanded the French garrison defending Jedburgh in 1548.

**Centre right:** The tower, which may have been used for accommodation when the canons' quarters were damaged beyond use.

**Below:** The abbey as it may have looked in 1548, when General d'Esse installed the defensive earthworks still known as 'The Ramparts'.

ANDRÉ DE MONTALEMBERT,
Comte d'Esse, Lieutenant Genéral pour le
Roi Commandant ses Armées en Ecosse Gouver-
neur de Teroane Mort sur la Breche de cette ville le 17 juin
1553.

During the later 1300s, the community, along with the nation, rebuilt its buildings and its wealth. The cloister was enlarged, and so too was the chapter house. In the 1400s, however, Jedburgh was again under fire. There were damaging attacks in 1409, when Jedburgh Castle was destroyed, and in 1410, 1416 and 1464. In 1476, the monastic buildings were said to be in need of repair. By 1502, the situation had reportedly worsened. The abbey church provides ample evidence of the major repair work undertaken by successive abbots between 1464 and 1520.

In 1523, an army led by the Earl of Surrey attacked and burned the abbey. The devastation must have been immense, for the community was driven to desperate measures. Roofs were lowered within the church and walls were built to restrict the church to an area below the crossing tower. It is possible that at least some of the domestic accommodation was too badly damaged to continue in use.

Two further attacks by English forces in 1544 and 1545 left the abbey once again badly damaged. The English occupied Jedburgh after their success at the Battle of Pinkie, near Edinburgh, in 1547, but from the spring of the following year a French force under the command of General d'Esse held the town. Since Jedburgh no longer had a castle and the only protection was the abbey precinct wall with its great towers, the French decided to fortify at least part of the abbey itself. This involved levelling some of the badly damaged buildings to create gun platforms and building an earthwork to protect the east flank of the abbey. This feature is now known as 'the Ramparts'.

---

## 1409

**JEDBURGH**
is attacked, and its castle is destroyed by the raiders. Three further major attacks follow, the last in 1464.

## 1523

**THOMAS HOWARD, EARL OF SURREY**
(who had defeated James IV at Flodden in 1513) attacks the abbey yet again, laying waste to much of the complex.

## 1548

**FRENCH FORCES**
under André de Montalembert, Comte d'Esse, occupy Jedburgh to defend it from the English.

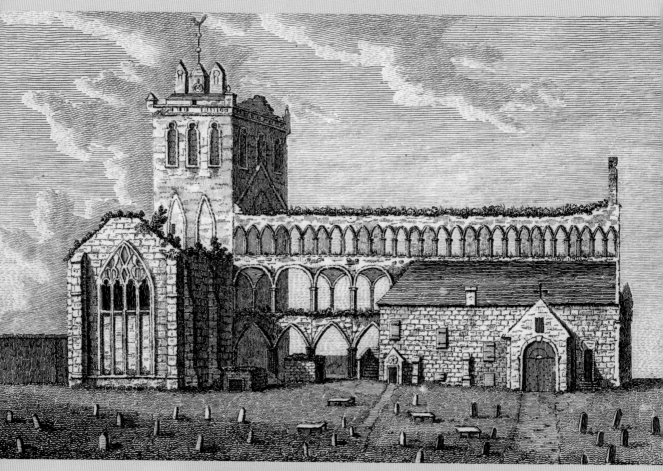

# THE REFORMATION AND AFTER

The canons had made considerable efforts to maintain a church in the crossing. This also enabled the abbey church to survive and continue as a parish church after the Reformation of 1560.

By this time, the community must have been quite small; it is unlikely that more than eight canons remained at the abbey. They were allowed to live out the rest of their days in their spiritual home, as long as they embraced the reformed religion.

A new parish church was formed in the remaining usable part of the abbey church, in the area beneath the central tower and transepts. By 1574, Privy Council records show that the roof of this section was decaying, and there were further problems in 1636 when one of the piers supporting the tower was judged to be at risk. The advice of the royal master mason, John Myln, was sought in 1642. His recommendations included significant demolition, but fortunately no action was taken. Between 1668 and 1671, perhaps due to concerns about the stability of the crossing area, a new church was established in the western part of the nave.

In 1681, much of the north transept was walled off and appropriated by the Ker family, ancestors of the Marquises of Lothian, who had long used it as their burial place. A manse and stables were built over the remains of the west range, and three houses constructed on the ruins of the east range. One of these later became a smithy. The SE corner of the cloister became the site of more mills, including a textile mill. In 1743, the vault over the church's crossing collapsed.

**Opposite top:**
An engraving of the abbey dated 1 December 1776. By this date, most of the abbey church lay derelict, but the parish church built into the northern wall of the nave was still in use and can be seen at the right.

**Opposite below, far left:**
Fragments of statues recovered at the site hint at the decorations that once enhanced the building. They are now on display in the visitor centre.

**Opposite below, center:**
A view into the north transept, which was partly walled off by the Ker family in 1681.

**Opposite below, right:**
A painting of the abbey by William Wilson, dated 1803.

## 1560  | 1668-71

**THE REFORMATION** transforms religious life in Scotland and many abbeys are abandoned. A few canons probably remain at Jedburgh, having embraced Protestantism.

**A NEW PARISH CHURCH** is built into the north wall of the nave.

## MARY SOMERVILLE (1780–1872)

Born in Jedburgh in 1780, Mary Somerville was a writer with a deep understanding of the emerging fields in science, astronomy and mathematics. In her youth, Mary visited her uncle in the Jedburgh manse, and he encouraged and supported her in her educational ambitions. The two would read Latin together before breakfast. Her work led to honorary membership of the Royal Astronomical Society, and she was among the first female scientists to receive such recognition. Her legacy lives on in the many objects and places named after her, ranging from a lunar crater to an island in the Barrow Strait, Northern Canada and Somerville College in Oxford.

**Top left:** A photograph taken around 1887 shows a mason standing in the restored doorway leading from the west end of the nave into the cloister.

**Above:** The choir of Jedburgh Old Parish Church, around 1880.

**Right:** The abbey church seen from Abbey Close, around 1870.

**Far right:** The east processional doorway in 1832, by which time it had been bricked up.

# RECENT TIMES

T he abbey has a long history of conservation work, dating from 1826, when public subscription paid for the strapping of the tower with iron bands set into the masonry.

A major turning point in the abbey church's modern history was the decision in 1875 to build a new parish church and manse on the far side of the Jed Water, largely at the behest of the 9th Marquis of Lothian. The parish church that had stood in the nave since 1671 was carefully dismantled, and the western end of the south aisle wall rebuilt. This work was accompanied by the clearance of various walls and buildings, including the manse, which had encroached on the cloistral buildings. The marquis paid for major repairs to the ancient fabric of the church, and in 1913 Jedburgh became the first of the great border abbeys to be placed into State care.

Such was the scale of the repair work to the abbey church that thoughts did not turn to excavating and laying out the cloister buildings until the 1930s. Little of the cloistral buildings remained above ground until clearance excavations in 1936–7. These removed some of the demolition debris and landscaping deposits, exposing the wall foundations for public display. However, a public road, The Bow, had been superimposed on the surviving remains of the undercroft and reredorter in the southern part of the site.

The viability of removing The Bow was assessed and agreed, and in 1984 a major programme of archaeological excavation began unravelling the complex sequence of building of the cloister ranges. It also uncovered some remarkable finds. In 1986, the abbey's new visitor centre was formally opened by Michael Ancram, the Scottish Office minister then responsible for ancient monuments and, coincidentally, a descendant of the 9th Marquis of Lothian.

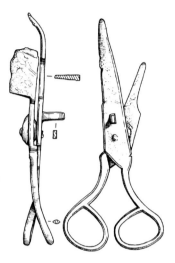

**Above:** A pair of candle-snuffers, probably 18th or 19th-century, found in the manse garden.

### THE 'OLD' PARISH CHURCH
is built across the Jed Water, sponsored by the 9th Marquis of Lothian, who also restores the abbey.

### MAJOR EXCAVATIONS
reveal the cloister and other outbuildings between the abbey church and the Jed Water.

# Jedburgh Abbey is one of a dozen Historic Scotland properties in the Scottish Borders, a selection of which is shown below.

## MELROSE ABBEY

Established in 1136 as a modest Cisterican monastery, Melrose Abbey was destroyed by Richard II in 1385, but much of its magnificent replacement survives.

↗ In Melrose, off the A7 or A68

🕐 Open all year

📞 01896 822562

🚗 Approx. **10 miles** from Jedburgh Abbey

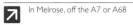

## DRYBURGH ABBEY

Despite three major fires and four military sieges, this Premonstratensian abbey is remarkably complete, still retaining some of its 12th-century features.

↗ On the B6404, near St Boswells

🕐 Open all year

📞 01835 822381

🚗 Approx. **8 miles** from Jedburgh Abbey

## SMAILHOLM TOWER

Built as a tower-house for the Pringles around 1430, remote Smailholm has survived reiving and the 'Rough Wooing' to retain its spectacular charm.

↗ In Smailholm village, north of Jedburgh on the A6089

🕐 Open all year
**Winter:** open weekends only

📞 01573 460365

🚗 Approx. **15 miles** from Jedburgh Abbey

## HERMITAGE CASTLE

Isolated and intimidating, Hermitage dominated Liddesdale for centuries, witnessing bloody violence, treasonable pacts and a royal romantic tryst.

↗ 5.5 miles NE of Newcastleton on the B6399

🕐 Open summer only

📞 01387 376222

🚗 Approx. **20 miles** from Jedburgh Abbey

For more information on all Historic Scotland sites, visit **www.historic-scotland.gov.uk**
To order tickets and a wide range of gifts, visit **www.historic-scotland.gov.uk/shop**

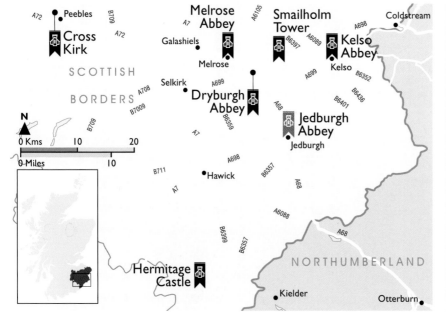

| Key to facilities | |
|---|---|
| Bus/coach parking | 🚌 |
| Car parking | 🅿 |
| Interpretive display | |
| Reasonable wheelchair access | ♿ |
| Shop | |
| Toilets | 🚻 |
| Self-serve tea and coffee | |
| Strong footware recommended | |
| Picnic area | |